Winslow Homer, 1836-1910 : Eastman Johnson, 1824-1906 : [exhibition]

Fine Arts Society of San Diego (Calif.)

appreciative and buying public. Many honors and awards, climaxing in a gold medal received at the Chicago World's Fair Exhibition in 1893, were bestowed upon him during his lifetime

Winslow Homer died in his studio at Prout's Neck, at the age of 74, on September 29, 1910.

If labels must be attached to a painter, the following three should be given to Homer naturalist, American, individualist

In accordance with the naturalistic spirit of the time, Homer believed that painting is the art of seeing He said: *"When I have selected the thing carefully, I paint it exactly as it appears."* Like other naturalists, he depicted contemporary life and people around him, and consequently his art was often considered ugly and revolutionary.

Homer was an American painter *par excellence*. His development as an artist parallels that of the American nation: starting with an early note of healthy optimism and occasional naïveté, and gradually acquiring maturity and depth. With realism Homer recorded the American soldier at the front, with sympathy and directness he painted the American youth at play, with a note of positive affirmation he portrayed the physical activity of the American people at work in the fields and at outdoor sports. With delicacy and joviality he observed the more fashionable and idyllic aspects of country life — the American *fête galante*.

Above all, however, Homer loved and understood nature. He was at his greatest when running the whole gamut of moods from lyrical gentleness to dramatic tension he painted nature or man's relation to it. His first-hand knowledge of the subject saved him from academic darkness, from becoming too sentimental or too literary It was to the everchanging aspects of the sea that he turned for comfort in a period of growing misanthropy. And it was nature again, this time the tropics, which released the puritanical severity of the old Yankee into a sensuous feast of warm and dazzling hues.

In the course of his development Homer followed with determination only one direction — his own. Though self-taught, his career was one of hard discipline and work Like so many painters he went abroad and visited France, the cradle of artistic innovation But unlike others he remained proudly immune to outside influences. In England, the traditional source of study for many American painters, he was impressed not by the art, but by the people and the climate of the country

In his direct painting on location which he learned as a correspondent, and in his interest in the varied atmosphere and moods of nature, Homer approaches Impressionism Light was for him as for Impressionists, an important factor, but he never allowed it to become his main concern, and never allowed it to dissolve or break forms. Whatever his relation to Impressionism, it was not one of direct influence. Endowed with vigor an unspoiled freshness and a bold honesty of vision in his canvass   ally in independent and individual painter

PAINTINGS

1 THE INITIALS

canvas, signed and dated lower left *Homer — 64*
16 x 12⅛ inches

REPRODUCED *Antiques,* Dec 1944, v 4b, p 356
Worcester Art Museum, *News Bulletin & Calendar,* 1944, v 10, p 2
New York, Wildenstein, *Loan Exhibition of Winslow Homer,* Feb 19-March 22, 1947, p 42, No 1

CATALOGUED *Catalogue of the Fortieth Annual Exhibition of the National Academy of Design,* N Y , 1865, No 577, p 33
Downes, William Howe, *The Life and Works of Winslow Homer,* Boston, 1911, p 276
Bolton, Theodore, "The Art of Winslow Homer, an estimate in 1932," *The Fine Arts.* February 1932, p 52
Bolton, "Homer Revisited at the Whitney," *Art News,* Oct 15-31, 1944, v 43, p 17
New York, Wildenstein, *op cit ,* p 32, No 1

CITED Worcester, Art Museum, *Winslow Homer,* Nov 16-Dec 17, 1944, No 3
Downes, William Howe, *op cit ,* p 276

EXHIBITED 1865, New York, National Academy of Design, No 577
1944, New York, Whitney Museum of American Art, Exhibition of Oils and Watercolors by Winslow Homer, October 3-November 2
1944, Worcester, Mass , Worcester Art Museum
1947, New York, Wildenstein, Loan Exhibition of Winslow Homer

In his book on Homer, Goodrich writes *"With his keen eye for fashion he delighted in the hoofeskirts, flounces, puffed sleeves, little round turbans, flying ribbons, and all the feminine absurdities of this unstreamlined day . . "* (Lloyd Goodrich, *Winslow Homer,* McMillan, New York, 1944, p 28).

The author also points out that the painter, one of the first interpreters of the American girl, created the 'Homer Girl' who, like the later Gibson girl, was a type rather than an individual. In *The Initials* one of these elegant and attractive beings, "the dashing brunette," is engaged in the romantic occupation of carving letters into the bark of a tree The light blue curve of the girl s dress is contrasted against the vertical darkness of the tree trunk The solidity of structure is combined with decorative qualities; the Ionic motive of embroidery on the dress adds a formal touch and the branches provide an overall delicate rhythm

2. SHARPSHOOTERS

canvas, signed and dated lower left *Homer '66*
17⅛ x 13⅛ inches

CATALOGUED New York, Wildenstein, *Loan Exhibition of Winslow Homer,* 1947, p 32, No 5

EXHIBITED 1947 New York, Wildenstein, Loan Exhibition of Winslow Homer
COLLECTIONS Garvan estate

In this work Homer's lack of interest in the human being as an individual is characterized by the position of the two sharpshooters with their backs turned to the spectator The emphasis here is on design, the geometric richness of the movement of figures, and the linear arrangement of the guns is thoroughly exploited As in *The Initials,* the volume of the figures forms a contrast to the light decorative background foliage

3. THE RETURN OF THE GLEANER

canvas, signed and dated lower left *Winslow Homer*, 1867
24⅛ x 18⅛ inches

REPRODUCED Watson, Forbes, *Winslow Homer*, New York, 1942, p 104
Andover, Mass, Phillips Academy, Addison Gallery of American Art, *American Paintings from the Collection of Stephen C Clark*, May 11-June 30, 1940, p 3
New York, Wildenstein, *Loan Exhibition of Winslow Homer*, Feb 19-March 22, 1947, p 41, No 8

CATALOGUED
Watson, Forbes, *op cit*, p 104
Andover, Mass, *Ibid*
New York, Wildenstein, *op cit*, p 32, No 8

CITED Hayes, Bartlett, "Collection of U S Painting, 1845-1929," *Art News*, June 1, 1940, vol 38, p 10 —
"One of Mr Clark's Homers, the *Return of the Gleaner* (painted in France, 1867, and, to the best of available information, never publicly exhibited and therefore little known) dovetails logically with the other three Homers in the exhibition The point is occasionally made that Homer, a complete individualist, was totally unaffected by his sojourn in France A comparison of *Croquet* and the *Morning Bell* (one painted before his trip, the other possibly so) with *Weaning the Calf*, which was painted afterward, certainly leads one to agree with this conclusion However, when the kinship of the *Return of the Gleaner* to the Barbizon school is considered, one feels that Homer is nevertheless a painter who is aware of the style and feelings of others about him "
Andover, Mass, *op cit*, Introduction p 3
"The four paintings by Winslow Homer from Mr Clark's collection all represent early phases of his work *Return of the Gleaner*, painted in France, in 1867, may have been inspired by Millet and the Barbizon school, with which Homer's early work has a decided kinship'

EXHIBITED 1940, Andover, Mass, Addison Gallery of American Art
1947 New York, Wildenstein, Loan Exhibition of Winslow Homer

COLLECTIONS
E T Webb, Webb City, Mo (1912)
Harry Jones, Kansas City, Mo (1919)
Mrs Julia Jones Lind (daughter of Mr Jones), Greenwich, Conn (1937)
Stephen C Clark, New York

The honest realism of Homer is well exemplified in the sturdy peasant woman approached with little idealization. A very satisfactory feeling of happy stability permeates the painting. The figure of the gleaner is treated in broad, almost cubic forms. She is firmly placed against the horizontal of the field and her own verticality is gently relieved by the diagonal of the hayfork and the movement of the windblown skirt

4 YOUNG GIRL AT A WINDOW

canvas, signed and dated lower left *Winslow Homer* 1873
19⅝ x 13¼ inches

COLLECTIONS Mrs Harry H Darst (née Grace Cullen), Franklyn, Ohio

Homer is always credited with a sense of design. This can best be seen in works like *Young Girl at the Window*. An almost oriental flatness is heightened by the profile position of the figure. The decorative pattern of forms is extremely varied, yet there is a strange austerity in spite of this surface wealth, brought about by the large dark plane of the window and the strict geometric organization of the

5 THE COTTON PICKERS

canvas, signed and dated lower left *Winslow Homer N A* 1876
24 x 38 inches

REPRODUCED *American Art News* —, p 1
Catalogue of Paintings by Eminent American Old Masters —, p 29
New York, Wildenstein, *Loan Exhibition of Winslow Homer*, Feb 19
March 22, 1947, p 48, No 19
Pictures on Exhibit, New York, March, 1947, p 5

CATALOGUED· *Catalogue of Paintings by Eminent American Old Masters and
by Some of the Prominent Living American Artists from the Collection
of Young's Art Gallery*, Chicago, 1918, p 28, No 16
Bolton, Theodore, 'The Art of Winslow Homer an Estimate in 1932,"
The Fine Arts, February, 1932, p 53
New York, Whitney Museum of American Art, *Winslow Homer Cen-
tenary Exhibition*, December 15, 1936-January 15, 1937, No 13, p 21
The Index of Twentieth Century Artists, Nov 1933, I, No II, p 8,
"Winslow Homer'
New York, Wildenstein, *op cit*, p 33, No 19

CITED. Downes, William Howe, *The Life and Works of Winslow Homer*,"
Boston, 1911, p 89
"Another negro picture which was the outcome of the journey to
Virginia in 1876 was the "Cotton Pickers," representing two stalwart
negro women in a cotton field This canvas (about thirty by forty
inches) (24 x 38) in a scale of browns and silvery grays was exhibited some time in the seventies at the Century Club, of which,
by the way, Homer was a member An English gentleman saw it
there, bought it, and took it to England, and Mr. F Hopkinson
Smith, who has sent me this information, together with a rough
sketch of the composition, thinks that the picture is practically
unknown in America
American Art News, XV, December 9, 1916, No 6, p 1 —
"The exceptionally good example of Winslow Homer, 'The Cotton
Pickers,' reproduced on this page, is now in an exhibition of some
36 choice modern American pictures ..
"This picture was painted in 1876 and soon afterwards went to
England where it was owned for a number of years by a wealthy
English cotton spinner The late Hopkinson Smith discovered it in
recent years and through his information, the picture came back to
America, and was purchased by Dr C B Guinn
"Mr W H Downes mentions the picture in his work on Winslow
Homer, but was unable to obtain a reproduction of the canvas"

Benezit, *Dictionnaire des Peintres et des Sculpteurs*, Paris 1924, Vol II,
p 636 (Sale 1st of April 1911)
Thieme, Ulrich and Becker, Felix, "Winslow Homer," *Allgemeines Lexi-
kon der Bildenden Kuenstler*, Leipzig, 1924, XVII
Breuning, Margaret, "Greatness of Homer Seen Anew at Whitney," *Art
Digest*, October 15, 1944, p 8
Goodrich, Lloyd, *Winslow Homer*, New York, 1944, p 59
Encyclopaedia Britannica, "Homer Winslow," Fourteenth Edition, Vol XI,
p 699
Pictures on Exhibit, New York, March 1947, p. 4

EXHIBITED 1878, London Royal Academy
187--, New York, Century Club
1918, Chicago, J W Young Galleries
1937, New York, Whitney Museum of American Art, Dec 15, 1936-
Jan 15, 1937, No 13
1944, New York, Whitney Museum of American Art, October 3-Novem-
ber 2
1947, New York Wildenstein, Loan Exhibition of Winslow Homer

COLLECTIONS English private collector
    Dr C B Guinn, Carthage, Missouri

"Homer had always been interested in Negroes, from Civil War day, and he was one of our first artists to get away from the old minstrel-show conception of the colored people and paint them with understanding and realism   ." (Lloyd Goodrich in the catalogue, *Loan Exhibition of Winslow Homer*, Wildenstein, New York, 1947).

It is in *Cotton Pickers* that Homer transcended the realm of genre-painting and gave a foretaste of the epic greatness and breadth of concept of his late seascapes. There is monumentality in these superbly modeled figures looming against the atmospheric landscape The two Negro girls present a repetition of a statement with subtle variations in their pose, their gestures, their outline One involuntarily is reminded of the laundresses of Degas This similarity is carried further by the subtle color harmonies of cool greys and warm brown. But in this painting Homer went beyond Degas and caught the individual differences of facial expression The two girls reflect opposed psychological attitudes· one a lazy animal like indifference, the other an alert, angry concentration The subtle divergence of texture and design is carried consistently into such details as the basket and bag, or the growing cotton

Homer seldom came as close to a heroic concept of Americana

6 ENCHANTED

canvas
11½ x 19 inches

CATALOGUED Lloyd Goodrich, Catalogue of Homer's Work (in preparation)

COLLECTIONS Townsend, Mass, member of the Homer family
    W Townsend, Mass, Mrs Margaret Christian

One of Homer's delightful representations of childhood, devoid of sentimentality is his canvas of two boys stretched out on the grass There is a disarming charm in the rounded outline of the boy's cheek and a little decorative touch in the two flowers on his hat A simplified cubic form of the barn and broad treatment of the figures contribute to a general simple statement of youth outdoors

7 FISHERFOLK, TYNEMOUTH

canvas
c 1881-1882
16 x 22½ inches

DOCUMENTED Letter of Charles L Homer (nephew of Winslow Homer)

CATALOGUED Pittsburgh, Pa, *Catalogue of the eleventh annual exhibition at the Carnegie institute, April eleventh to June thirteenth, nineteen hundred and seven*, No 221 (?)
    San Francisco, Calif, Panama Pacific International Exposition *Catalogue de luxe of the department of fine arts* . editor John E D Trask, San Francisco, 1915, I, No 2517, p 197, II, No 2517, p 325
    Macbeth Gallery, N Y, *Winslow Homer exhibition*, May-June, 1938, No 16
    New York, Wildenstein, *Loan Exhibition of Winslow Homer*, Feb 19-Mar 22, 1947, p 33, No 23

CITED Downes, William Howe. *The life and works of Winslow Homer*,

Exhibited 1907, Pittsburgh, Pa , Carnegie institute, No 221
1912, Boston, Mass , Doll and Richards, February
1915, San Francisco, Calif , Panama-Pacific exposition, No 2517
1923, Boston, Mass , Doll and Richards, January
1938, New York, Macbeth gallery, May-June, No 16
1947, New York, Wildenstein, Loan Exhibition of Winslow Homer

Collections Mrs. Charles Savage Homer (sister-in-law of Winslow Homer)
Mr Charles L Homer (nephew of Winslow Homer)

Homer's work at Tynemouth shows a greater preoccupation with atmosphere and light and an added depth in his concept of the human being. *"He first began to picture the sea, and the men and women who made their living on it. His fashionable young ladies were things of the past; these fishergirls were sturdy outdoor women who could do a man's work ."* (Lloyd Goodrich in the catalogue, *Loan Exhibition of Winslow Homer*, Wildenstein, New York, 1947).

The women flanking the doorway caught in a momentary action of knitting or gossiping, possess the solidity of structure and permanence of existence of northern caryatids. There is some genre element in playing children and cats, and an element of still-life in the arrangement of pots, pans, barrels and baskets Most of all there is a presence of light contributing towards a fuller modeling and giving a general happy and cheerful note to the whole.

WATERCOLORS

"It is a curious fact that Homer did not begin to work regularly in watercolor, of which he was to be one of the greatest modern masters, until he was thirty-seven, in 1873 The medium suited him perfectly from the first. He was essentially a draftsman and a recorder of the external world In watercolor he could work directly from nature, proceeding from a pencil sketch to a finished picture in color at one sitting In this medium he made discoveries—of places, subjects, light, color — that he later embodied in oils .

"Homer's watercolors introduced a new breadth and boldness into watercolor painting Up to this time most work in the medium had been in the old style of finished representation — essentially colored drawing. But Homer brought to watercolor the spirit of impressionism — concentration on visual sensations, broad handling, bold simplification, daring color . . No watercolorist of the time approached him in technical mastery, in breadth and brilliancy of washes, in the unerring sureness with which the picture was built up from the first pencil indications to the last firm brushstroke He was a master of every trick of the craft, always keeping the medium pure and transparent.

" .. Always he retained solidity of form ; and always he spoke in the direct sensuous language of line, color and pattern, and not by illusion His watercolors were not only masterly as representations, they were also superb as decoration, with their linear beauty and their magnificence of color

"Our greatest watercolorist of the period, he revolutionized the vision and technique of watercolor painting in this country, and became the father of today's vigorous American watercolor school Almost every leading watercolorist since his day, no matter how far removed from Homer's direct naturalism, owes something to his achievement " (Lloyd Goodrich, in the catalogue, *Loan Exhibition of Winslow Homer*, Wildenstein, New York, 1947.)

8. WAVERLY OAKS
watercolor
1880
9 x 13¼ inches

CATALOGUED New York, Wildenstein, *Loan Exhibition of Winslow Homer*, Feb 19-March 22, 1947, p 36, No 51

EXHIBITED 1947, New York, Wildenstein, Loan Exhibition of Winslow Homer

9. SMALL SLOOP IN GLOUCESTER HARBOR
water color, signed lower right *Homer*
c 1880
9½ x 13¼ inches (sight)

REPRODUCED Prouts Neck, Prouts Neck Association, *Winslow Homer*, 1936, No 11

CATALOGUED Prouts Neck, Prout's Neck Association, *Ibid.*
Macbeth Gallery, New York, Introduction to Homer, Dec 15, 1936-Jan 18, 1937, No 54
New York, Wildenstein, *Winslow Homer — Watercolors and Drawings*, Summer 1948, No 13

CITED Carlyle Burrows, *New York Herald Tribune*, June 6, 1948
Howard Devree, *New York Times*, June 6, 1948

EXHIBITED 1936, Prout's Neck, Maine, Prout's Neck Association
1936-37, New York, Macbeth Gallery
1948, New York, Wildenstein, Winslow Homer — Watercolors and Drawings

COLLECTIONS Private collection, Boston

10. FIVE BOYS ON THE BEACH
water color, signed and dated lower right *Winslow Homer* 1880
6 x 13 inches

CATALOGUED: New York, Wildenstein, *Winslow Homer — Watercolors and Drawings*, Summer 1948, No 9

EXHIBITED 1881, New York, American Water Color Society
1948, New York, Wildenstein, *op cit*, No 9

COLLECTIONS H S Rubens
Mrs Joan Rogers

11 THREE BOYS
watercolor
1880
7 x 13½ inches

CATALOGUED New York, Wildenstein, *Loan Exhibition of Winslow Homer*, Feb 19-March 22, 1947, p 36, No. 52
New York, Wildenstein, *Winslow Homer — Watercolors and Drawings*, Summer 1948, No 10

EXHIBITED 1881, New York, American Water Color Society
1947, New York, Wildenstein, Loan Exhibition of Winslow Homer
1948, New York, Wildenstein, Winslow Homer — Watercolors and Drawings

COLLECTIONS H S R

12. BOY FISHING FROM A BOAT

water color, signed and dated lower right *Homer* 1880
9 x 12⅞ inches (sight)

CATALOGUED New York, Wildenstein, *Loan Exhibition of Winslow Homer*,
Feb 19-March 22, 1947, p 36, No 53
New York, Wildenstein, *Winslow Homer — Watercolors and Drawings*,
Summer 1948, No 11

EXHIBITED 1936, Cambridge, Fogg Museum of Art
1938, Cambridge, Fogg Museum of Art
1941, Cambridge, Fogg Museum of Art
1947, New York, Wildenstein, Loan Exhibition of Winslow Homer
1948, New York, Wildenstein, Winslow Homer — Watercolors and
Drawings

COLLECTIONS Mrs William Harris Arnold, Cambridge
Mr Weld Arnold

"These watercolors (done in 1880) were obviously painted outdoors They were informally composed His chief interest was evi-
dently in light and nature's changing effects Surrounded by this
great expanse of water and sky, he attacked problems of luminosity
as he never had before . " (Lloyd Goodrich, *Winslow Homer*,
McMillan. New York, 1944, p 67 (cf. Nos 9-12.)

13. BIG TREES, ADIRONDACKS

watercolor, signed upper left *Homer*
c 1889
13½ x 19½ inches

CATALOGUED New York, Wildenstein, *Loan Exhibition of Winslow Homer*,
Feb 19-March 22, 1947, p. 37, No 66

CITED Robert Coates, "Man from Maine," *New Yorker*, March 1, 1947

EXHIBITED 1947, New York, Wildenstein, Loan Exhibition of Winslow
Homer

COLLECTION Charles B Homer

"Homer was an inveterate hunter and fisherman, and almost
every summer he and his elder brother Charles made a camping trip
to the northern woods — to the Adirondacks in the late 1880's and
early 1890's and later to Quebec On these trips he combined sport
and art, painting many watercolors, almost all of them done direct
from nature . Homer's viewpoint, as always, remained objective
He saw nature less as a poet than a woodsman, expressing not poetic
sentiments but physical sensations. He conveyed the vivid, direct
sensation of the stillness of the deep forest, the black depths of lake
water, the shy beauty of deer, the exhilaration of the mountaintop,
the wild freshness of all this unspoiled world His watercolors seem
specimens of nature, closer to that great primal source than any other
art of their time " (Lloyd Goodrich, in the catalogue *Loan Exhibition
of Winslow Homer*, Wildenstein, New York, 1947, p 27.)

14. NASSAU. WATER AND SAILBOAT

water color, signed lower left *Winslow Homer*, Feb'y 1899
14⅞ x 15½ inches

REPRODUCED· New York, Macbeth galleries, *Winslow Homer, water colors
and early oils*, May-June 1938, No 4
Art Digest, March 15, 1937
New York Herald Tribune, June 6, 1948

CITED. Carlyle Burrows, *New York Herald Tribune*, June 6, 1948
Howard Devree, *New York Times*, June 6, 1948

CATALOGUED New York, Macbeth galleries, *Ibib*
New York, Wildenstein, *Loan Exhibition of Winslow Homer*, Feb. 19-
Mar 22, 1947, p 38, No 80
New York, Wildenstein, *Winslow Homer — Watercolors and Drawings*,
Summer 1948, No 16

EXHIBITED 1934, Cleveland, Museum of Art
1938, New York, Macbeth galleries
1947, New York, Wildenstein, Loan Exhibition of Winslow Homer
1948, New York, Wildenstein, Winslow Homer — Watercolors and
Drawings

COLLECTIONS Given by Homer to member of the family of former owner,
Laurence F Peck
Private Collection

15. BLACK BASS, FLORIDA

water color, signed lower left *Homer* 1904
19⅜ x 10⅞ inches

REPRODUCED Prout's Neck, Maine, Prout's Neck Association, *Winslow
Homer centenary loan exhibition*, 1936, pl. 15
World Telegram, July 27, 1939

CATALOGUED. Prout's Neck, Maine, Prout's Neck Association, *op cit.*, No 15
New York, Macbeth galleries, *Introduction to Homer*, Dec 15, 1936-
Jan 18, 1937, No 64
New York, Wildenstein, *Loan Exhibition of Winslow Homer*, Feb. 19-
March 22, 1947, p 38, No 84

EXHIBITED 1936, Prout's Neck, Maine, Prout's Neck Association
1937, New York, Macbeth galleries
1947, New York, Wildenstein, Loan Exhibition of Winslow Homer

COLLECTION Charles B Homer

From 1898 Homer went often to the Bahamas or Florida (Nos.
14 & 15). "We may note that it was about this time that Gauguin
was also discovering his earthly paradise in the South Seas It is re-
markable that Homer was in his middle sixties when he painted these
watercolors, so young in freshness and energy In these late southern
watercolors Homer attained his greatest brilliancy of color The trans-
parency of the medium, with the white paper showing through, gave
them a luminosity he never achieved in oil . . ." (Lloyd Goodrich
in the catalogue, *Loan Exhibition of Winslow Homer*, Wildenstein,
New York, 1947).

DRAWINGS

Homer was essentially a draftsman. His training as a reporter was
responsible for his swift and selective rendering of essentials In his crayon
studies a moving pattern of contrasting planes and lines provides a variety
of design. White splashes of chalk accent the crispness of his drawing
The textural richness is further heightened by Homer's use of brown
paper

16. GIRL RESTING

drawing on brown paper, signed and dated lower right *Homer* 1872
7 x 8¼ inches

CATALOGUED New York, Wildenstein, *Winslow Homer — Watercolors and
Drawings*, Summer 1948, No 1

CITED Emily Genauer *New York World Telegram* June 8, 1948

EXH   N   Y   Winslow Homer   Watercolors

17. SHEPHERDESS
drawing, signed and dated lower left *Homer* 1878

9 x 13 inches

REPRODUCED New York, Parke-Bernet Galleries, *John F Kraushaar* sale,
April 9-10, p 2, No 6

CATALOGUED New York, Parke-Bernet Galleries, *Ibid.*
New York, Wildenstein, *Winslow Homer — Watercolors and Drawings,*
Summer 1948, No 4

EXHIBITED 1935, New York, Macbeth Galleries
1948, New York, Wildenstein, Winslow Homer — *Watercolors and*
Drawings

COLLECTIONS Winslow Homer Estate
Horace D Chapin, Boston
Sargeant Collier, Boston

18. GIRL PICKING APPLES
drawing on brown paper, signed lower right *W H.*

c 1878

7 x 8¼ inches

CATALOGUED New York, Wildenstein, *Loan Exhibition of Winslow Homer,*
Feb 19-March 22, 1947, p 39, No 95
New York, Wildenstein, *Winslow Homer — Watercolors and Drawings,*
Summer 1948, No 6

EXHIBITED 1947, New York, Wildenstein, Loan Exhibition of Winslow
Homer
1948, New York, Wildenstein, Winslow Homer — Watercolors and
Drawings

19. UNDER THE APPLE BOUGHS
drawing on brown paper, signed lower left *Homer*

c 1878

9 x 14½ inches (sight)

Note A similar sketch is in the Cooper Union collection (7 11/16 x 5 9/16
inches, given by Charles Savage Homer, 1878-79)

CATALOGUED New York, Wildenstein, *Winslow Homer — Watercolors and
Drawings,* Summer 1948, No 5

EXHIBITED 1948, New York, Wildenstein, Winslow Homer — Watercolors
and Drawings

20 THE REAPER
pencil and white chalk on brown paper
signed and dated lower left· *Winslow Homer* 1879

8¾ x 14¼ inches (sight)

REPRODUCED New York, Parke-Bernet, *Mrs George A Martin sale,* Oct 18,
19, 1946, No 113

CATALOGUED New York, Macbeth gallery, *Introduction to Homer,* Dec 15,
1936-Jan 18, 1937, No 11
New York, Parke-Bernet galleries, *Ibid*
New York, Wildenstein, *Loan Exhibition of Winslow Homer,* Feb 19-
Mar 22, 1947, p 39, No 96
New York, Wildenstein, *Winslow Homer — Watercolors and Drawings,*
Summer 1948, No 8

EXHIBITED 1936/1937, New York, Macbeth gallery
1947, New York, Wildenstein, Loan Exhibition of Winslow Homer

1948, New York, Wildenstein, Winslow Homer — Watercolors and Drawings

COLLECTIONS: Mrs Woodruff J. Parker, Chicago
Mrs George A. Martin

21 THROUGH THE FIELDS

black crayon on tan paper heightened with white
signed lower left. *Winslow Homer*, dated illegibly

1879
10 x 15 inches

REPRODUCED· New York, Parke-Bernet galleries, *Mrs George A Martin sale*, Oct 18, 19, 1946, No 114

CATALOGUED. New York, Parke-Bernet galleries, *Ibid.*
New York, Wildenstein, *Loan Exhibition of Winslow Homer*, Feb 19-Mar 22, 1947, p. 39, No 97
New York, Wildenstein, *Winslow Homer — Watercolors and Drawings*, Summer 1948, No 7

EXHIBITED 1947, New York, Wildenstein, Loan Exhibition of Winslow Homer
1948, New York, Wildenstein, Winslow Homer — Watercolors and Drawings

COLLECTIONS Mrs. Woodruff J Parker, Chicago
Mrs George A. Martin   .

22. MULE RIDER

pencil and white chalk on brown paper
signed and dated lower right. *W. H* 1885

8¼ x 9 inches (sight)

REPRODUCED Boston, Goodman & Walker, Inc, *Exhibition of Old Prints and Paintings*, Nov 1936, List I, No 59, p. 8

CATALOGUED Boston, Goodman & Walker, Inc, *op cit*, List I, No. 59
New York, Parke-Bernet galleries, *Mrs George A. Martin sale*, Oct 18, 19, 1946, No 111

EXHIBITED. 1936, Boston, Goodman & Walker, Inc

COLLECTIONS Purchased from the artist
Mr Sweet
Miss Nina Sweet, his daughter
Mrs George A Martin

THE LIFE AND ART

OF

EASTMAN JOHNSON

Eastman Johnson was born in Lowell, Maine, in August 1824 His father's career as Secretary of State of Maine forced the family to move several times during the boy's childhood From 1834 to 1839 the Johnsons stayed in Augusta, where the boy's formal schooling was rather vague, and he spent most of his time exploring the country with his numerous brothers and sisters. The year 1839 found Johnson in Concord, New Hampshire, employed in a country store Already at this early stage he showed great interest in, and ability for drawing, and used his spare time to make sketches of the local people.

In 1841 he was placed in a lithographer's shop in Boston, perhaps Bufford's, where later Homer was to get an education By 1842 Johnson back in Augusta, set up a studio and established himself as an independent portraitist, working probably in pencil. His father's connections provided him with sitters, among them members of the State legislature. In 1844-45 Johnson moved to Washington, D. C, where opportunities for portraiture proved even greater, and such important personalities as Mrs Alexander Hamilton, "Dolly" Madison, and Daniel Webster came to pose for the twenty-two year old artist His portraits had the popularity of today's photographs, and many a time he was asked to make copies.

Johnson, however, must have been subject to a certain restlessness, for in the summer of 1846 he moved to Boston There his stay of three years was again marked by considerable success, his first and most faithful client being Henry Wadsworth Longfellow.

Virtually self-taught until now, in 1849 Johnson went abroad to study in Germany. Accompanied by a friend, he settled in Duesseldorf, at that time a popular place with art students He worked under Emanuel Leutze (the painter of "Washington crossing the Delaware") and was heartily welcomed by his German colleagues who, for the first time, elected an American artist a member of their club.

The years from 1849-51 were spent at The Hague, a stay which proved to be of extreme importance for Johnson's stylistic evolution. His own work was very popular with the Dutch as well as with the American colony in Holland In 1855 Johnson went to Paris for a short while and he studied with Couture, but this visit made little impression on the painter.

Upon his return to America, Johnson undertook his first trip to Wisconsin, there he stayed from 1856 until January 1857, painting the Indians settled around the Great Lakes. He returned once more the same year to continue recording "frontier life "

Soon afterwards Johnson went to Cincinnati, doing high-price portrait commissions, and in 1859 he went for a trip to the South Around this time he finally settled in New York. Here, the exhibition of his painting *Old Kentucky Home* (cf, No 1) was a great success, and in 1860 he was elected to the National Academy. During the Civil War Johnson followed the Union Army, sketching battle scenes and life at the front

In the early '70's Johnson married Elizabeth Buckley and moved to an apartment uptown, his residence, until his death It was also in the '70's that he discovered Nantucket and spent several summers on the island where he produced some of his best pieces After 1887, Johnson forsook genre painting for portraiture. His last period of hard and remunerative work was interrupted by three European trips which had, however, little influence on his painting.

Eastman Johnson died in New York in 1906

The relationship between the two painters Homer and Johnson is still an open question. it could be both, an interesting example of parellel growth, or a case of mutual influence in their development toward freer, more atmospheric painting. The artists knew each other and were both members of the Academy about the same time. Undoubtedly they must have seen each other's work. Like Homer, Johnson resisted French influence Like Homer he followed the army during the Civil War in search for subjects, unlike Homer, however, he did not paint on the spot, but worked from sketches in his studio. In his deeply rooted realism, directness and honesty, in his portrayal of the American scene, Johnson also approached Homer. But in his interest in and his extensive recording of Indians and in his studies of Negroes, done directly from life, Johnson was a pioneer.

Johnson began his apprenticeship as a draftsman in a lithographer's workshop. In Duesseldorf he perfected his drawing and received a good academic basis in anatomy, composition and perspective In The Hague he was overwhelmed by Rembrandt and, after a period of copying, he finally absorbed and digested on his own level the art of this master with such success that he earned for himself the nickname of "The American Rembrandt." From this great teacher Johnson learned the significance of light. But it is perhaps more just to call Johnson an "American small master." In the present exhibition he is represented as a painter of *genre,* a field in which — like the Dutch 17th century small masters — he excelled One of Johnson's friends and critics said of him *"Although from the first, he took up these genre subjects many years ago from pure love of them."* (Brooklyn Museum, *An American Genre Painter, Eastman Johnson,* 1940).

Johnson painted small-town life, country life, days of work and days of festivity, the landscape and the people he loved and knew best. His painting is a record of Americana, conceived with authenticity and flavor, but it has a a qu ty as well as purely pictorial values

Childhood, a preoccupation characteristic of the art and letters of the period, is a favorite theme with Johnson, as with the young Homer. His "Little Men" and "Little Women" are members of a happy and healthy society A work such as *Freedom Ring* (No 11) does not convey to today's spectator any feeling of the social or historic importance of the event, but merely a warm sympathy for a child playing with a new toy

Johnson's approach is often emotional, sometimes frankly sentimental, at other times narrative, but his simple, unsophisticated work, never photographic, trivial, or distasteful, is like a refreshing breeze.

That Johnson knows how to handle paint becomes evident when one compares the rich, strong colors of *Work at the Fair* (No 10), or *Rock-A-Bye-Baby* (No. 6) with the subdued, delicate color harmony of *The Woodsman Eating* (No 13).

Johnson is a skilled draftsman, and his sense of pattern can best be seen in *The Early Scholar* (No 4). The almost abstract arrangement of different forms gives an air of detached objectivity and an awareness of design to a canvas which could have easily become a merely visual anecdote.

The atmosphere of warmth and intimacy, that marks many of Johnson's interiors, is to be found also in out-of-doors scenes, as in the case of *Southern Courtship* (No. 1). Johnson's taste and sense of proportion is best visible in works like *A Lullaby* (No. 5) or *Work for the Fair* (No 10), where figures and still-life are well balanced, Johnson never allows his love of detail to be overpowering

Johnson's painting cannot always be dated on purely stylistic grounds. There is a difference between his earlier tightly knit, delineated and descriptive compositions, like *Southern Courtship* (No. 1), and the more panoramic views of his Fryeburg series, (No 14), there is a difference between his handling of light and paint in the warm, sunny *Courtyard* (No. 12), the dark shadows, reminiscent of the Dutch of *About Right* (No 7) and his impressionistically conceived Nantucket scenes (Nos 16 & 17) But next to these later landscape and figure pieces of the '70's, airy and luminous, bold in spirit and execution, there are paintings like *Child Playing with Rabbits* (No 15), dated 1876 In it Johnson returns to the solidity of modeling, to his interest in formal organization, to a more detailed realistic approach, here light, though an important factor, is used again to build up, not to dissolve Thus Johnson's development is not one of strict continuity

John J. H Baur, Curator of the Brooklyn Museum, in his catalogue of "An American Genre Painter, Eastman Johnson," (1940) says of Johnson's painting· *"As its best it rose entirely above sentimentality of any kind and was strong, clean painting in a peculiarly native idiom. There are enough of these better paintings . . I believe, to entitle him to a place in the growing gallery of American old masters."*

"It seems likely . . that the discoveries of Homer and Johnson were made independently, although they may have mutually reinforced each other In any case, they both represent the advance guard of a new and n trne trend in American painting, the impact of which is still being felt to.1 "

PAINTINGS

1 SOUTHERN COURTSHIP, study for MY OLD KENTUCKY
HOME
canvas, signed and dated lower right *E Johnson* 1859
20 x 15¾ inches
>This painting is a finished study for Johnson's famous *Old Kentucky Home*, exhibited with great success at the National Academy in 1859

CATALOGUED New York, Wildenstein, *Eastman Johnson*, Summer 1948, No 2

CITED Carlyle Burrows, *New York Herald Tribune*, June 6, 1948

EXHIBITED 1948, New York, Wildenstein

2 THE LITTLE SENTINEL
canvas board, signed and dated lower left *E Johnson* '62
9⅜ x 7⅜ inches

3 TASTING THE SAP
oil on academy board, signed lower right *E J*
1865-73
15¾ x 9⅞ inches
>This figure appears with variations in several canvases of the Fryeburg series

4. THE EARLY SCHOLAR
canvas board, signed and dated lower left *E Johnson* 1865 (or 1868?)
17 x 21 inches

REPRODUCED *Christian Science Monitor*, May 17, 1948

CATALOGUED New York, American Art Galleries, *Eastman Johnson sale*,
Feb 26-27, 1907, No 113
Brooklyn Museum, *An American Genre Painter — Eastman Johnson*, 1940,
p 40 (95)
New York, Wildenstein, *Eastman Johnson*, Summer 1948, No 6

CITED· *Art News*, Summer 1948, p 49

EXHIBITED 1948, New York, Wildenstein

COLLECTIONS Eastman Johnson
W. J. Curtis

5 A LULLABY
oil on academy board, signed and dated lower left. *E. Johnson* 1864-9
16⅜ x 13⅜ inches

CATALOGUED Brooklyn Museum, *Eastman Johnson*, 1940, p 65, No 120
New York, Wildenstein, *Eastman Johnson*, Summer 1948, No 5

EXHIBITED 1948, New York, Wildenstein

COLLECTIONS Dr Hyatt Lyke

6 ROCK-A-BYE, BABY, ON THE TREE TOPS
canvas, signed lower left *E J*
c 1856-57
19¾ x 15¾ inches

CATALOGUED Brooklyn Museum, *Eastman Johnson*, 1940, p. 61
New York, American Art Galleries, *Eastman Johnson sale*, Feb 26 27,
1907, No 61
New York, Wildenstein, *Eastman Johnson*, Summer 1948, No 13

EXHIBITED 1948, New York, Wildenstein

COLLECTIONS Eastman Johnson
Misses F Pearl and Elizabeth Browning

7 ABOUT RIGHT
panel, signed and dated lower right *Eastman Johnson* 1863
15 x 12¾ inches (sight)

CATALOGUED New York, Wildenstein, *Eastman Johnson*, Summer 1948, No 4
EXHIBITED 1948, New York, Wildenstein

8 GLOUCESTER BOY
oil on academy board, signed lower left *E Johnson*
14 x 7¾ inches

CATALOGUED New York, American Art Association, *Eastman Johnson sale*,
    Feb 26-27, 1907, No 83
    New York, Wildenstein, *Eastman Johnson*, Summer 1948, No 11
EXHIBITED 1948, New York, Wildenstein
COLLECTIONS Mrs Eastman Johnson

9. MOTHER FEEDING HER CHILD
canvas
15 x 12½ inches

CATALOGUED New York, Wildenstein, *Eastman Johnson*, Summer 1948, No 8
EXHIBITED 1948, New York, Wildenstein

10. WORK FOR THE FAIR
canvas, signed and dated lower left *E Johnson*, Dec 25, 1862
16¾ x 20¾ inches

REPRODUCED *Pictures on Exhibit* June, 1948, p 9
CATALOGUED New York, Wildenstein, *Eastman Johnson*, Summer 1948, No 3
EXHIBITED 1948, New York, Wildenstein

11. THE FREEDOM RING
canvas, signed lower left *E Johnson*
c 1860
17¾ x 21¾ inches

REPRODUCED New York, American Art Association, *Thomas Hitchcock &*
    Others sale, Mar. 17-20, 1914, No 181
    New York Sun, June 25, 1948

CATALOGUED Brooklyn Museum, *An American Genre Painter — Eastman*
    Johnson, 1940, p 39, p 64, No 101
    New York, American Art Association, *Ibid*
    New York, Macbeth Gallery, Americana, Nov 1-30, 1939, No 15
    New York, John Levy Galleries, *Eastman Johnson Exhibition*, April 8-30,
    1942, No 21
    New York, Wildenstein, *Eastman Johnson*, Summer 1948, No 1

CITED Walton, William, "Eastman Johnson, Painter," *Scribner's*, vol 40,
    1906, pp 272-273 —
        "In 1860 a runaway slave girl was sold at auction in Plymouth
        Church by Henry Ward Beecher, to obtain funds to purchase her
        freedom, and was brought by Mr Beecher to Mr Johnson for her
        portrait, a photograph of which, representing her in rapt admiration
        of a ring given by a lady as a contribution to the fund, is still in
        Mrs Johnson's possession "

EXHIBITED 1860 New York, National Academy of Design, No 449
    1939, New York, Macbeth Gallery
    1940, Brooklyn Museum
    1942, New York, John Levy Galleries
    1948, New York, Wildenstein
COLLECTIONS Thos Hitchcock

12. THE COURTYARD

canvas, signed lower left *E. J*

12 x 14 inches

CITED *Art News,* Summer 1948, p 49

CATALOGUED New York, Wildenstein, *Eastman Johnson,* Summer 1948,
No 15

EXHIBITED 1948, New York, Wildenstein

13 STUDY OF A WOODSMAN EATING

oil on academy board

1865-73

13¼ x 10⅝ inches

CITED *Art News,* Summer 1948, p 49

CATALOGUED New York, Wildenstein, *Eastman Johnson,* Summer 1948, No 9

EXHIBITED 1948, New York, Wildenstein

14 CARD PLAYING AT FRYEBURG, MAINE, or
MAPLE SUGAR CAMPFIRE, FRYEBURG, MAINE

canvas, signed lower right *E Johnson*

1865-73

18⅞ x 29⅛ inches

REPRODUCED New York, Metropolitan Museum of Art, *Life in America,*
Apr 24-Oct 29, 1939, p 117, No 156

CATALOGUED New York, Metropolitan Museum of Art, *Ibid*
Brooklyn, N Y, Brooklyn Museum of Art, *Eastman Johnson,* Jan 18-
Feb 25, 1940, p 62, No 44, p 42 No 41 —
"This (like No 44 and Nos 45, 47, 48, below) is a "finished
study" for one of the incidents in the large composition of the
maple sugar festival which Johnson projected (see Nos 42 and
49-51, pp 43, 44) The whole series is said to have been done
near Fryeburg, Maine "
New York, Whitney Museum of American Art, *A Century of American
Landscape Painting,* 1800-1900, Jan 19-Feb 25, 1938, p 27, No 29
New York, Frazier gallery, *Eastman Johnson exhibition,* Sept -Oct, 1937,
p 5, No 14
New York, American Art Gallery, *Eastman Johnson sale,* Feb 26-27,
1907, No 70
Springfield, Springfield Museum of Fine Arts, *A Century of American
Landscape Painting,* 1800-1900, Mar 8-28, 1938, p 27, No 24
New York, Wildenstein, *Eastman Johnson,* Summer 1948 No 10

CITED Carlyle Burrows, *New York Herald Tribune,* June 6, 1948

EXHIBITED 1937, New York, Frazier gallery
1938, New York, Whitney Museum of American Art
1938, Springfield, Museum of Art
1939, New York, Metropolitan Museum of Art
1948, New York, Wildenstein

COLLECTIONS· Eastman Johnson
Frances P Garvan, Wheatley Hills, New York

15 CHILD PLAYING WITH RABBITS

oil on academy board, signed and dated lower right *E Johnson* 1876

29 x 24¾ inches

REPRODUCED Alonzo Lansford, *Art Digest,* July 1, 1947

CATALOGUED New York, Wildenstein, *French and American Nineteenth
Century Painting.* Summer 1947, No 16
New York Wildenstein *Eastman Johnson* Summer 1948 No 7

CITED Alonso Lansford, *Ibid*
Howard Devree, *New York Times*, June 29, 1947

EXHIBITED: 1947, New York, Wildenstein, French and American Nineteenth
Century Painting
1948, New York, Wildenstein

16. CRANBERRY PICKERS

oil on academy board, signed lower right. *E. J*
painted in 1876 at Nantucket
19½ x 30 inches

REPRODUCED Crosby, Everett U, *Eastman Johnson at Nantucket*, Mass,
1944, p 26, No C 8

CATALOGUED Brooklyn Museum, *An American Genre Painter — Eastman
Johnson*, 1940, p 62, No 57
Cambridge, Fogg Museum of Art, *Art in New England; New England
genre*, May 15-Sept 1, 1939, p 39-40, No 18 —
" Painted in 1876 at Nantucket where cranberry growing is an
important agricultural industry Johnson called this and others in a
similar loose technique "finished sketches."
Crosby, Everett U, *op cit*, p. 13, No C 8
New York, Frazier Gallery, *Eastman Johnson exhibition*, Sept -Oct,
1937, No 19 —
"The *Cranberry Pickers*. It is too bad that Johnson did not remain
with this impressionistic expression In but few strokes he captures
the entire movement of a group of people engaged in simple occu-
pation By strong but subtle highlighting of their actions The treat-
ment of the composition, in a series of planes, reminds one of
Breughel, in his series of the 'Seasons.'"
New York, Knoedler & Co, *Paintings & Drawings by Eastman Johnson*,
Jan 7-26, 1946, No 11
New York, John Levy Galleries, *America in the 19th century*, May 16-
June 9, 1944, No 1

EXHIBITED 1937, New York, Frazier Gallery
1939, Cambridge, Fogg Art Museum
1944, New York, John Levy Galleries
1946, New York Knoedler & Co

COLLECTIONS: Mrs Eastman Johnson
Norman Hirschl
Thomas N Metcalf

17 BERRY PICKERS

oil on academy board, signed lower right *E J*
1870-76
11½ x 22 inches

REPRODUCED Crosby, Everett U, *Eastman Johnson at Nantucket*, 1944, pl
p 28, No. C. 10

CATALOGUED Crosby, Everett U, *op cit*, p 13
New York, John Levy Galleries, *Eastman Johnson*, April 8-30, 1942,
No 15
Brooklyn Museum, *Eastman Johnson*, 1940, p 62, No 52
New York, Wildenstein, *Eastman Johnson*, Summer 1948, No 14

CITED *Art News*, Summer 1948, p 49

EXHIBITED 1942, New York, John Levy Galleries
1948, New York, Wildenstein

COLLECTIONS Norman Hirschl
Thomas Metcalf